GOODBYE Old FRIEND

A PICTORIAL ESSAY

on the Final Season at
Old Comiskey Park

written by
Frank Budreck

edited by
John Regnier

Published by Aland Corporation

Published by Aland Corporation

Layout and Design by Shepelak Design Associates, Inc.

Edited by John Regnier

Illustrations by Tim McWilliams

Color Separation by Digicon Graphics, Inc.

Photography by Frank Budreck

Printed in the United States of America

First Edition

Library of Congress Catalog Card Number: 91-73448

ISBN   0-9630204-0-4

ALAND CORPORATION
4125 South Joliet Avenue
Lyons, Illinois 60534

II

This book is
dedicated to all of the fans, players,
umpires, members of the media,
park personnel and all others who
made Old Comiskey what it was.

Acknowledgments

I wish to thank the White Sox organization and Major League Baseball for their assistance in putting this project together, all players on the White Sox and other teams who have made the 1990 season extra special, Richard Goggin for his seemingly endless groundwork efforts, Bob Leska, John Furlan, John Thorn, Michael Grossman, Kate Farrell, Jackie Fitzgerald, and the Tooke Family for their helpful opinions and expert advice, Larry Martin and Jack Jehezian for their professional photo printing, our illustrious tour guide and White Sox aficionado, Ralph Wick, Carol Husiak and John Sopcak for their help in carrying camera equipment throughout the park, and all the other people that make this endeavor possible by their appearance within this book.

Picture Credits

The Boston Red Sox: 40 lower right; 67 upper

The Coca-Cola Company: 35 upper left

Nancy Faust: 87; 146

Andy Frain Services: 6 both; 92; 93 lower right; 94 lower left

Hillerich & Bradsby: 129 "Reprinted with the permission of Hillerich & Bradsby Company, Louisville, Kentucky"

Carol Husiak: 33 lower right

Major League Baseball Properties and the Chicago White Sox:
VIII; 11 upper right; 13 both; 40 lower right; 50; 67 upper; 75 top and bottom; 85 right; 118 both; 128 lower right; 129; 144; 145 lower left; 147 lower right

Major League Umpires Association: 40 lower right; 67 upper

Mitsubishi America: 34 both; 35 lower right

Arthur Musinski: 123

Rawlings Sporting Goods: 10; 59 right; 67 lower right; 91 lower left; 103 right; 104; 105 upper right

Andy Rozdilsky: 90; 91 upper right; 157 lower left

Score Baseball Card Company: 121 upper right

Sportservice Corporation: 7; 107; 108 both; 109; 110; 111 both; 113 both; 114; 115 right; 116; 118 both

Topps Company, Inc.: 22 right; 103 upper left

Table of Contents

Introduction:
Memories of Comiskey Park

Old Comiskey Park...the time-honored "cathedral" at 35th and Shields...the "Baseball Palace of the World"...the old ball yard. Built on top of a junkyard in 1910, more than 72 million White Sox fans have passed through Comiskey's turnstiles in 80 years.

Countless fans will tell you they "grew up" here. Some can recall the exact date their father took them to their first game. Others simply remember the excitement and awe of their first trip to the major league ball park.

Comiskey Park has provided vivid memories that have withstood the passage of time... all-star and world series games... the Black Sox...the Go-Go Sox... the South Side Hitmen...the Winning Ugly Sox and more.

Remember the trip across the street to McCuddy's Tavern that is just as old as Comiskey? Stand up to the bar and wonder if you are standing in the exact place where Babe Ruth, Bill Veeck and other favorites have stood.

Old Comiskey Park was much more than just a building. There was a certain mystique about Comiskey. It was a special place — a true, oldtime ball park. The

**The excavator takes
a bite out of McCuddy's
— March 27, 1989**

sheer massiveness of its arched windows and history-saturated walls could leave you spellbound.

And who will ever forget that...well...interesting shade of green paint that detailed Comiskey Park and, quite often, a few of the neighboring front porches?

And remember that thrill, each and every time, of walking up the dark, cavernous entrance ramps to emerge and catch that first glimpse of the sun-drenched baseball diamond?

More than just a ball park, Comiskey Park was an experience. If you listen carefully, you can still hear the national anthem starting each game, the organ music playing popular tunes, the vendors' cries, Andy the Clown's cheers, booing the ump, the crack of the bat, the roar of the crowd, the oohs, the ahhs, the na na na na hey hey hey goodbyes.

Close your eyes. Can you taste that terrific variety of ethnic food? The hot dogs? The beer? Can you feel the discarded peanut shells crunching under your shoes? Can you still sense that musty dampness that always seemed to lurk under the seats?

Do you remember sloshing through the flooded washrooms or getting a shoeshine under the stands? How about sitting patiently through rain delays while energetic fans slide across the tarp? Sitting near you are groups of sailors on leave and, on those warm, humid summer nights, can you still see the ever-present cloud of cigar smoke hovering under the arc lights?

Then there is the rush of the crowd at game's end. You patiently shuffle your way like cattle down the exit ramps until you're finally outside the park, only to get a whiff of bus exhaust up your nose and the shriek of police whistles in your ear.

Your car is hopelessly blocked in the "quick exit" parking lot, so you resign yourself to watching the fireworks from your front seat. And you

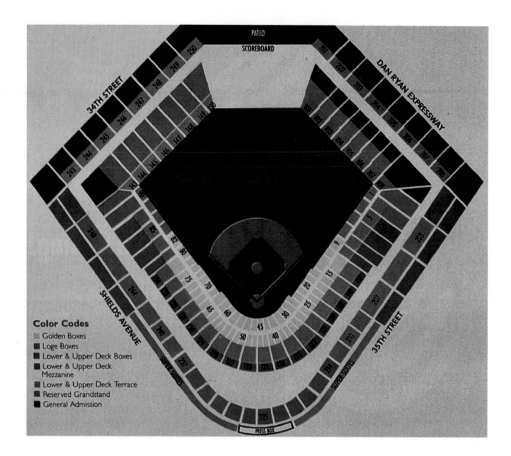

Color Codes
- Golden Boxes
- Loge Boxes
- Lower & Upper Deck Boxes
- Lower & Upper Deck Mezzanine
- Lower & Upper Deck Terrace
- Reserved Grandstand
- General Admission

wouldn't trade this moment for anything.

Baseball games can certainly be enjoyed in spacious new stadiums with modern facilities and expensive "sky boxes," but the true character of baseball still rests in the old ballyards, like Comiskey, with their rusty girders and aging bricks.

Comiskey Park aged gracefully for 80 years until it was the oldest major league park in use. Finally, progress threw her a curve.

Hopefully, new Comiskey Park will prove to be an excellent setting for the next 80 years of Chicago White Sox games and a new generation of fans will start creating their own special memories. But, for now, we want to say "goodbye" to our old friend.

Old Comiskey Park has been torn down to create a parking lot for the new stadium. It now exists only in photographs and in memories. Hopefully, this collection of photographs from the final season at Comiskey Park will enhance your special memories of the Grand Old Lady for years to come.

GOODBYE OLD FRIEND

For eighty years they came. First by trolley and by carriage. Later by elevated train and by car. More than 72 million White Sox fans converging on the "cathedral of baseball" at 35th and Shields. The air outside the ball park was always electrified with pre-game excitement and the shouts of parking attendents and curbside vendors. Welcome to historic Comiskey Park.

4

As White Sox fans arrive by foot and by car, they are greeted by the ever-present parking attendants and street vendors.

Fans make their way to the ball park down 35th Street.

6

The turnstiles spin as fans enter Comiskey Park. Total attendance for the 1990 season was 2,002,359, almost double the previous year's attendance.

7

The first stop for any devoted fan is to pick up a program and scorecard.

One youngster brings his glove to the park in hopes of catching a foul ball (left).

The stroll up the ramps (below) is Comiskey Park's answer to providing fresh air and exercise for the fans.

Eager fans arrive early to await batting practice home run balls in the right field stands. Over the years, many shins have been bruised bumping into Comiskey's inflexible wooden seats while fans scrambled for loose balls.

APRIL 9TH

Opening Day Marks Beginning of End for Old Comiskey

Thanks to a 32-day spring training lockout of players by baseball's team owners, the 1990 baseball season starts a week late. A damp, 51-degree Comiskey Park opens its gates for its final Opening Day on April 9.

Most baseball prognosticators have picked the White Sox to finish dead last in the American League West Division. Despite the gloomy weather and the gloomier predictions, hopes run high throughout the old ball park (as they always do on Opening Day) as 40,008 faithful fans gather to take their seats.

Fifty years ago this month, the only Opening Day no-hitter in baseball history occurred right here at Comiskey. Pitcher Bob Feller and the Cleveland Indians defeated the White Sox on April 16, 1940, by a score of 1 to 0. Fortunately, the 1990 Sox hitters will fare much better in today's opener.

A short rain delay postpones the start even further, but following the traditional player introductions, Charles A. Comiskey II, the grandson of White Sox founder Charles A. Comiskey, throws out the ceremonial first pitch. The White Sox soon take the field with Melido Perez on the mound. Perez will be opposed by pitcher Chris Bosio of the Milwaukee Brewers.

Nancy Faust, the ball park's organist, is playing "Suicide is Painless." Home plate umpire Rich Garcia begins the final season at Old Comiskey with the familiar cry of "play ball," and the game gets underway at 2:17 p.m.

The first hit of the game comes in the Milwaukee second inning when veteran Dave Parker singles to right field. The first Sox hit of the new season also comes in the second as

First pitched ball of the 1990 season by Melido Perez to Milwaukee's Gary Sheffield. It was a little low for ball one.

Carlton Fisk knocks a double into the left field corner.

Milwaukee's lone run for the day comes in the third inning when catcher B.J. Surhoff doubles to drive in Edgar Diaz from first base.

The Sox tie the score in the fifth inning when shortstop Ozzie Guillen scurries home from third base on a wild pitch. Guillen had led off the inning with a triple.

Third baseman Robin Ventura leads off the Sox seventh with a walk. Sammy Sosa bunts safely, putting runners at first and second. Guillen also bunts, but lead runner Ventura is thrown out at third base. Lance Johnson *also* lays one down and the bases fill up with Sox runners as the Brewers are frustrated, watching the slow-rolling bunt come to a standstill just inside fair territory along the third-base line. Scott Fletcher's sacrifice fly to right field brings Sosa home with the go-ahead run.

This series of events to manufacture a critical run will typify the scrappy, competitive nature of the 1990 Sox team and gives the fans their first taste of the many exciting, close games the team will play this season.

EVENT CODE
SOX0402 SEC147 LL 1 A
PRICE 6.50 LOWER DECK RGS PRICE 6.50
SEC147
CA 297x
LL SEAT 1
SOX1152
A19JAN0
GAME #1
CHICAGO WHITE SOX
- VS -
MILWAUKEE BREWERS
COMISKEY PARK
MON APR 2 1990 1:30 PM

11

April 2nd ticket honored April 9th.

Early arrivals to the start of the final season at Old Comiskey Park.

Bobby Thigpen is called on in the ninth to finish the game and he chalks up his first save of 1990, which will prove to be a record-setting year for the young reliever.

As the last Milwaukee batter is retired, the Comiskey scoreboard fills the air with the triumphant explosions of victory fireworks.

Pitcher Barry Jones records the win as the White Sox defeat the Brew Crew 2-1. After one day of play, the Sox sit atop the A.L. West Division with a perfect record of 1 and 0. The fans' optimism felt at the beginning of the game is rewarded and will prove to be continually buoyed throughout the 1990 baseball campaign. ■

A light rain falls on the jubilant Opening Day crowd following the White Sox' victory. The skeletal structure of the new Comiskey Park across the street has already begun to take shape.

1990 White Sox Coaching Staff

Jeff Torborg (Manager)	Herm Schneider (Trainer)
Barry Foote	Mark Anderson (Assistant Trainer)
Terry Bevington	Willie Thompson (Sox Clubhouse Manager)
Ron Clark	Joe McNamara (Visitors Clubhouse Manager)
Sammy Ellis	Gabe Morell (Asst. Visitors Clubhouse Manager)
Walt Hriniak	Vince Fresso (Umpire Equipment Manager)
Dave LaRoche	Steve Odgers (Conditioning Coach)
Joe Nossek	Glen Rosenbaum (Traveling Secretary)

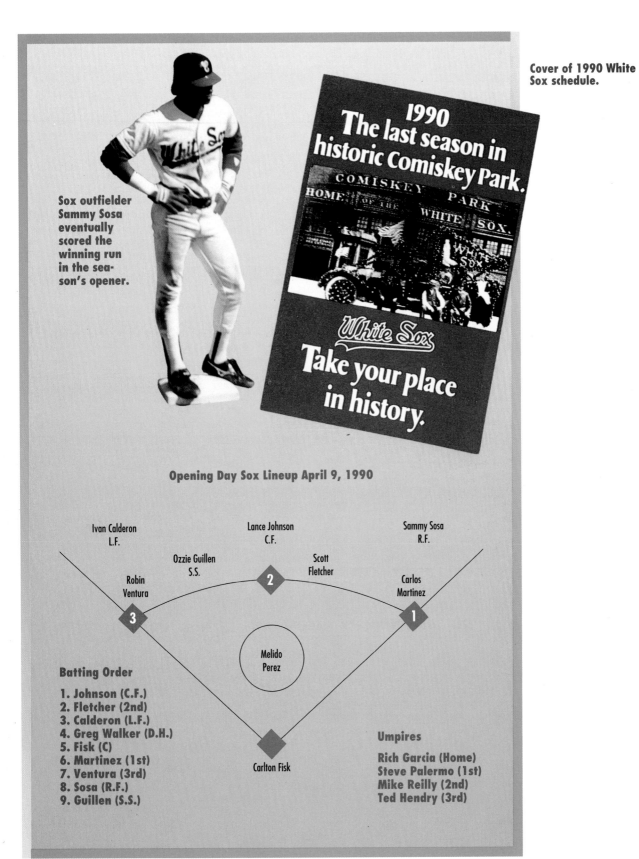

Cover of 1990 White Sox schedule.

Sox outfielder Sammy Sosa eventually scored the winning run in the season's opener.

1990 The last season in historic Comiskey Park.

COMISKEY PARK
HOME OF THE WHITE SOX.

White Sox

Take your place in history.

Opening Day Sox Lineup April 9, 1990

Ivan Calderon
L.F.

Lance Johnson
C.F.

Sammy Sosa
R.F.

Ozzie Guillen
S.S.

Scott
Fletcher

Robin
Ventura

Carlos
Martinez

2

3

1

Melido
Perez

Batting Order

1. Johnson (C.F.)
2. Fletcher (2nd)
3. Calderon (L.F.)
4. Greg Walker (D.H.)
5. Fisk (C)
6. Martinez (1st)
7. Ventura (3rd)
8. Sosa (R.F.)
9. Guillen (S.S.)

Carlton Fisk

Umpires

Rich Garcia (Home)
Steve Palermo (1st)
Mike Reilly (2nd)
Ted Hendry (3rd)

BASEBALL PALACE OF THE WORLD

At the turn of the
century, most baseball parks were
unsafe, wooden structures that held
fewer than 5,000 people. Fans quite
often had to stand behind ropes on
the actual playing field. So when
White Sox owner Charles Comiskey
commissioned architect Zachary
Taylor Davis to build his dream arena,
it was considered the most magnifi-
cent and safest park ever built. When
Comiskey Park opened on July 1, 1910,
it was immediately heralded as "The
Baseball Palace of the World."

16

When built in 1910, Comiskey Park was only the third "modern" concrete-and-steel ball park in the United States.

The White Sox ticket office (below) proved to be a very busy place in 1990.

Originally constructed on top of a junkyard, Comiskey Park rose from such humble beginnings to welcome more than 72 million fans through its gates over a period of eight decades.

18

By 1990, Comiskey Park was the oldest baseball park still in use in the major leagues.

CHICAGO

19

Comiskey Park
acquired its white
coat of paint and
distinctive green
trim in 1959, thanks
to owner Bill Veeck.

The brick relief C's
(below) were added
to Comiskey's facade
in 1927.

20

The two Comiskey Parks stand side-by-side as a testament to Chicago's past and a portent of its future.

Two views from outside Comiskey: (left) the far side of left field, and (below) behind the second-generation exploding score-board – another Veeck innovation.

Kittle Blasts First Sox Homer
of Year Over Rooftop

O n the night of April 17, with temperatures in the mid-30s, the White Sox' Ron Kittle blasts what will be the last roofshot in Comiskey Park history before a chilled crowd of 8,479.

It comes in the sixth inning off Boston reliever Rob Murphy and is a prodigious 452-foot game-tying homer that lands between the two light standards on the left field roof.

The blast is also the long-awaited first home run for the White Sox this year. It is Kittle's seventh roofshot and the 44th in Comiskey Park history. The White Sox go on to defeat the Boston Red Sox 2-1.

"Copyright the Topps Company, Inc."

The bat Ron Kittle used to power his 452-foot roofshot (left).

ROOFSHOTS

Batter	Pitcher	Date
Babe Ruth (N.Y.)	Tommy Thomas	August 16, 1927
Lou Gehrig (N.Y.)	Urban "Red" Faber	May 4, 1929
Jimmie Foxx (Bos.)	Bob Cain	June 16, 1936
Hank Greenberg (Det.)	Bill Dietrich	April 21, 1938
Jimmie Foxx (Bos.)	John Rigney	May 14, 1940
Ted Williams (Bos.)	John Rigney	May 7, 1941
Eddie Robinson	Al Widmar (St.L.)	April 25, 1951
Mickey Mantle (N.Y.)	Billy Pierce	June 5, 1955
Ted Williams (Bos.)	Harry Byrd	July 23, 1955
Bill Skowron (N.Y.)	Billy Pierce	July 24, 1956
Minnie Minoso	Bud Daley (K.C.)	September 21, 1960
Elston Howard (N.Y.)	Ray Herbert	July 15, 1961
Dave Nicholson	Moe Drabowsky (K.C.)	May 6, 1964
Boog Powell (Balt.)	Juan Pizarro	July 18, 1966
Buddy Bradford	Tom Hall (Minn.)	April 25, 1969
Don Mincher (Oak.)	Bart Johnson	May 24, 1970
Tom Egan	Jack Brown (Wash.)	July 25, 1971
Harmon Killebrew (Minn.)	Dave Lemonds	July 1, 1973
Dick Allen	Mike Cuellar (Balt.)	May 1, 1973
Richie Zisk	Don Gullett (N.Y.)	June 4, 1977
Sal Bando (Oak.)	Wilbur Wood	August 28, 1977
*Greg Luzinski	Bryan Oelkers (Minn.)	June 26, 1983
*Greg Luzinski	Ray Fontenot (N.Y.)	August 1, 1983
*Greg Luzinski	Dennis Boyd (Bos.)	August 28, 1983
*Ron Kittle	Chris Codiroli (Oak.)	September 6, 1983
*Ron Kittle	Mike Walters (Minn.)	September 19, 1983
*Ron Kittle	Al Nipper (Bos.)	April 29, 1984
*Ron Kittle	Dave Rozema (Det.)	July 2, 1984
*Greg Luzinski	Jack Morris (Det.)	July 3, 1984
*Ruppert Jones (Det.)	Tom Seaver	July 3, 1984
*Ron Kittle	Bob Ojeda (Bos.)	August 1, 1984
*Carlton Fisk	Bob Ojeda (Bos.)	August 1, 1984
*Kirk Gibson (Det.)	Tom Seaver	May 10, 1985
*Carlton Fisk	Charlie Leibrandt (K.C.)	May 30, 1985
*Ron Kittle, Game 1	Bob Ojeda (Bos.)	August 8, 1985
*Harold Baines	Tom Filer (Tor.)	August 23, 1985
*George Bell (Tor.)	Tom Seaver	August 24, 1985
*George Bell (Tor.)	Floyd Bannister	August 25, 1985
*Brian Downing (Calif.)	Jerry Don Gleaton	September 18, 1985
*Jose Canseco (Oak.)	Joel Davis	September 22, 1985
Rob Deer (Milw.)	Tom Seaver	April 7, 1986
Larry Sheets (Balt.)	Bob James	May 9, 1987
Dan Pasqua	Frank Tanana (Det.)	May 30, 1989
Ron Kittle	Rob Murphy (Bos.)	April 17, 1990

*Roofshots hit while home plate was moved eight feet closer to the outfield.

When the upper deck of Comiskey was added in 1927, experts determined that a batter would have to hit a ball more than 474 feet on the fly to clear the roof — a feat thought impossible. Babe Ruth proved them wrong when he blasted a home run over the right field roof that year.

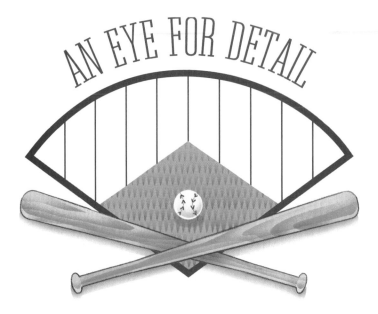

AN EYE FOR DETAIL

Anyone who has visited other baseball parks across the country knows that Old Comiskey Park was one of a kind. It was built specifically for baseball and bore little resemblance to many of the modern, "cookie-cutter" stadia. Longtime fans look back with fondness at the many individual qualities of the old ball yard. From the green C's on the facade to the arched windows, from the exploding scoreboards to the pre-World War II wooden seats, Comiskey was a unique and special place down to its tiniest details.

26

Architect Zachary Taylor Davis designed the famous Romanesque arched windows of Comiskey, which encouraged comparisons of the ball park to the Roman Coliseum in Italy.

Gate 8 (left) is closed for the evening.

Probably due to crowd flow consid-erations, Gate 3 (below) had been welded shut for years.

27

28

Comiskey was noted for its massive iron infrastructure.

Baseballs hitting Comiskey's ironwork (right) would often disperse roosting flocks of pigeons. Unwary fans below were frequently targets of the birds' excitement.

Fans pass beneath some of Comiskey's iron girders (below).

30

Charles A. Comiskey apparently decided to incorporate the support pillars into the grandstand's design as a cost-cutting measure, thus creating the somewhat controversial "obstructed-view seats."

Green plastic "con-
tour" seats were
added in 1982 for
the fans sitting in
the box seat sections.

32

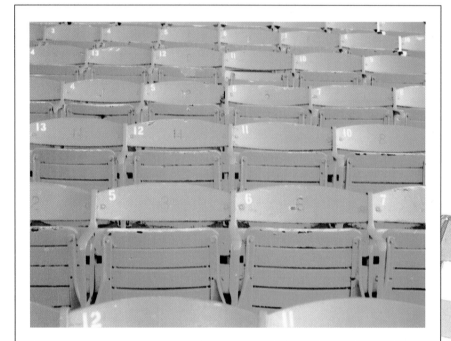

The painted numbers on these box seats don't always match the engraved numbers on the chairs, a testament to decades of seating renovations.

The last few rows (left) are as far away from the action as you can get.

If you look closely (below), you can see the original coat of red paint on these old, wooden seats.

33

34

Comiskey Park has always maintained a love affair with its scoreboards. Even the original 1910 manually operated scoreboard was an imposing wooden structure that dominated center field.

Seating expansion in 1927 necessitated the addition of two electronic auxiliary scoreboards built into the right and left field walls.

An electronic center field scoreboard, built in 1951, featured the sign "Chesterfield! It's a hit!" that lit up each time a Sox player got a base hit.

The first "exploding" scoreboard in baseball history (above) was the idea of Bill Veeck. His original "Monster" was built in 1960 and stood for 21 years. It featured lights, whistles, sirens, smoke and fireworks whenever a White Sox player hit a home run.

The Diamond Vision board (right) was constructed in 1982, bringing Comiskey Park into the modern television age.

36

RESALE OF TICKETS AT ANY PRICE IS PROHIBITED
PRESS / PASS GATE

**No more tickets will
be sold to games at
Old Comiskey Park.
How many fans
long for just *one
more game* here?**

Father's Day Game
Includes Visiting Mayors

Today is the last Father's Day Game here at Comiskey Park. It is also Mayor's Day and Chicago Mayor Richard M. Daley plays host to several mayors from other cities.

In an old-timers game that precedes the regular fare, the Sox Old-Timers lose to the Oakland Athletics Old-Timers.

Unfortunately, that game foreshadows the real game, in which the White Sox also lose to the Athletics, this time by a score of 5 to 2.

The Athletics are the current world champions of baseball and are heavily favored to win the A.L. West Division. They probably didn't suspect it yet, but the White Sox would end up being their strongest competitors of the 1990 season in the race for the division crown. ■

Oakland's Mark McGwire eyes an Adam Peterson offering.

A FAN'S EYEVIEW

With more than
40,000 seats to choose from, a White
Sox fan could view a home game
from any number of vantage points.
Behind home plate was a great place
to watch the pitcher, while the out-
field bleachers offered a chance at
the occasional home run ball. In the
sun or in the shade, close to the field
or high up in the top deck, Comiskey
Park offered an authentic baseball
experience to all of her fans.

40

One of the biggest benefits of a ball park built exclusively for baseball is that the fans can get close to the players, whether for autographs (left) or to witness the action.

First baseman Frank Thomas (below) holds Boston's Mike Marshall close to the bag while umpire Steve Palermo supervises.

Fans going to the park early get to watch the New York Yankees (above) taking batting practice.

This seat (right) is just barely in foul territory down the right field line.

42

View from the lower deck in left field (left).

A grandstand perch for a Chicago vs. Texas affair (below).

Television monitors (above) help fans follow the game from the dark and cavernous left field stands.

The upper deck from behind home plate (right) provides a scenic view of the field and the center field scoreboard.

44

Cross beams make viewing the third base line a challenge from these grandstand seats.

"I must be in the
front row!"

46

Peering through a window (left) at Comiskey's east parking lot, the main sign and the Dan Ryan Expressway.

These seats (below) offer a terrific view of Old Comiskey's steel and concrete, but not of the right field corner.

On a crowded,
sunny afternoon,
fans watch the
game from the
scoreboard ramp.

48

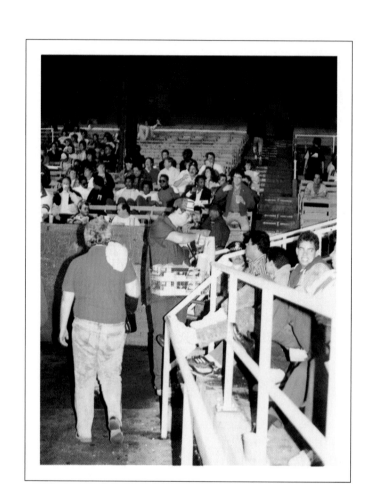

**A little corner of
heaven.**

You don't have to be an archeologist (left) to recognize what civilization has been here — baseball fans!

Welcome to the upper deck (below).

49

Yankee Pitcher Tosses No-Hitter– And Loses!

From the beginning, July 1 is not an ordinary day at Comiskey Park. It was 80 years ago today that the first game was played here and today also marks the final appearance by the New York Yankees, historically the most feared team over that 80 year span.

Andy Hawkins goes to the mound for New York while Greg Hibbard pitches for the White Sox. The game about to begin will, without a doubt, be the wildest one at Comiskey all year and sure to be featured on every sportscaster's highlight film tonight.

Hawkins maintains a perfect game until he issues two walks in the fourth inning. The innings pass quickly as Hibbard also pitches a perfect game until

the sixth inning, when he allows two infield hits, but no runs.

Dual shutouts are still being hurled by both pitchers and Hawkins still has his no-hitter intact when his trouble begins. In the eighth inning, with two outs, Sox batter Sammy Sosa dives safely into first base after Yankee third baseman Mike Blowers bobbles his grounder for the first Yankee error of the afternoon.

Ozzie Guillen and Lance Johnson walk to load the bases. Robin Ventura's deep fly to left field gets caught in the swirling winds and is dropped by outfielder Jim Leyritz for Yankee error number two. All three baserunners score.

Ivan Calderon hits a fly ball to right fielder Jesse Barfield, who, battling the sun and wind, also drops the ball. This third error of the inning allows Ventura to cross home plate with the fourth Sox run. Ironically, Hawkins has still not allowed a hit.

The calm before the storm.

51

The Yankees fail to score in the top of the ninth and the Comiskey Park crowd graciously applauds Hawkins, who has the bittersweet honor of pitching a no-hitter only to lose the game 4-0.

Oddly enough, Hawkins is not even the first Yankee pitcher to lose a no-hitter. The same fate also befell pitcher Tom Hughes in 1910 — the year Comiskey Park was opened. Hmmmm...

It is bizarre, exciting games like this one that make the baseball world begin to notice this team of "no-names" on Chicago's South Side and ask, "Who are these guys?" ∎

July 1, 1990 Boxscore

New York	ab	r	h	bi
Kelly cf				
Sax 2b	4	0	0	0
Mattingly 1b	4	0	0	0
Balboni dh	4	0	0	0
Tolleson pr	0	0	0	0
Je Barfield rf	4	0	1	0
Leyritz 1f	3	0	1	0
Blowers 3b	3	0	0	0
Geren c	3	0	1	0
Espinoza ss	2	0	1	0
Totals	31	0	4	0

WHITE SOX	ab	r	h	bi
L. Johnson cf	3	1	0	0
Ventura 3b	4	1	0	0
Calderon dh	3	0	0	0
Pasqua 1f	4	0	0	0
Kittle 1b	3	0	0	0
Lyons 1b	0	0	0	0
Karkovice c	2	0	0	0
Fletcher 2b	2	0	0	0
Sosa rf	3	1	0	0
Guillen ss	2	1	0	0
Totals	26	4	0	0

New York	000	000	000 — 0
WHITE SOX	000	000	04X — 4

E—Ventura 2, Blowers, Leyritz, Je Barfield. DP—WHITE SOX 1. LOB—New York 5, White Sox 3. SB—Sosa (14). S—Espinoza.

New York	HP	H	R	ER	BB	SO
Hawkins L, 1-5	8	0	4	0	5	3

WHITE SOX	HP	H	R	ER	BB	SO
Hibbard	7	4	0	0	0	4
B.Jones W, 10-1	1	0	0	0	0	1
Radinsky	1	0	0	0	0	0

PB—Geren. Umpires—Home, Scott; First, Voltaggio; Second, Reilly; Third, Meriwether. T—2:34. A—30,642.

How they scored

SOX EIGHTH—with two out, Sosa reached on Blowers' error. Guillen and Johnson walked. Leyritz dropped Ventura's fly in left, three runs scoring. Barfield dropped Calderon's fly in right, Ventura scoring. Four runs.

A FAN'S FAVORITE PLACES

Comiskey Park was a fan's ball park. And each fan had a favorite little nook or cranny of the old park that held a special memory. Comiskey's famous Picnic Area offered the only outfielder's-point-of-view-seating in the major leagues, as well as delicious food. And any "ball hawk" knows all the best places to grab a souvenir home run or foul ball. Comiskey's charm was the sum of its individual parts — the unique places and spaces tucked away throughout the park.

54

Comiskey's unique picnic areas were added in 1960 to accommodate large groups as well as to give fans an out-fielder's-eye-view of the game. The picnic areas were another Veeck idea.

A facsimile scoreboard welcomes guests to the patio area, located beneath the center field scoreboard.

56

Located under the right field stands, the Bullpen II was available for group rentals.

The unique configuration of Comiskey Park enhanced the acoustics so even fans sitting in the left field corner (left) could often hear the umpire's ball-and-strike calls. Conversely, the players on the field had no trouble hearing the cheers and jeers from the fans.

(Below) Deep right center field.

57

58

Although the out-field stands were dubbed "the cheap seats," the area was a good place to catch rays, as well as homers.

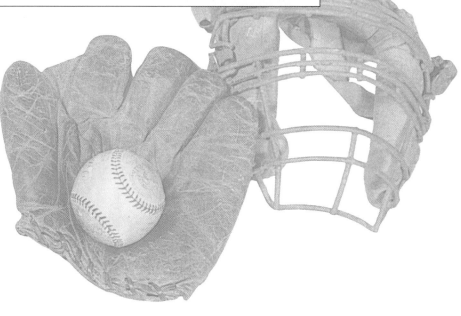

During games, high foul balls often went "up on the roof" and out of Comiskey onto the surrounding streets. There, a scramble for the prized ball usually ensued by a small group of regulars collectively labeled "The Ball Hawks."

When inside the ball park, this group of Sox faithful often could be seen moving quickly, yet gracefully, past bleacher obstacles to catch a batting practice home run ball. Some of their catches could rival any made on the playing field.

"Ball Hawk" John Witt (above) patrols 35th Street with a radio as his guide.

(Above right) Tar-stained "roof ball."

Crowd Pleasers: Millions of men found relief in Comiskey's *sanctum sanctorum* over the years. Although not especially attractive, the troughs proved efficient in handling the large, anxious crowds.

62

A pitching machine under the stands gives fans a chance to measure their throwing velocity and match it against baseball's fastest hurlers.

Hitting Display Lights Up Comiskey on Independence Day

Fireworks finally light up center field at 11:58 p.m., but they celebrate Independence Day rather than a White Sox victory.

A crowd of 23,547 endures the hot, humid, 96-degree evening to see the Sox' Jack McDowell start this 4½-hour marathon that is decided in the twelfth inning when the Sox lose to the Detroit Tigers 10-7.

Ken Patterson, the fifth Sox pitcher of the night, starts the twelfth inning and gives up two singles and a three-run home run to Detroit's Mike Heath. By game's end, Detroit has outhit Chicago 17 to 12.

White Sox manager Jeff Torborg, who was later named Manager of the year, has one comment, "Man, they can hit! Gee, that ball club can hit!" ■

63

The fireworks display celebrates the Fourth of July.

AUTHORIZED PERSONNEL ONLY

There were, of course, some places within the walls of Comiskey Park that the average fan was not allowed to go. Behind the doors marked "private" awaited another world not seen by the general public — a realm traveled only by the players, management and staff. Now is the last chance to glimpse a peek at that secret world behind Comiskey's closed doors.

66

"Hey – isn't that Frank Thomas?" The Sox rookie (left) walks past fans on his way to the batting cage located beneath the stands on the third-base side of Comiskey. This area was the best-kept secret in the park for autograph seekers (below).

After passing Thomas under the stands before the game, the fans can later see him in action on the field (above), here against the Boston Red Sox. It's a tribute to the up-close and personal feeling fans could get at Old Comiskey.

(Right) A Frank Thomas autographed ball.

68

This auxiliary
elevator tower
services the west
side of Comiskey.

Roofshots. **Here's two views from Comiskey's roofs. Note the television cables and new Comiskey Park (above).**

70

The Bards Room, (left) located behind the upper deck, offered complimentary food and drink to members of the press and special guests of the ball park. The room was renovated during the early 1980s.

The White Sox weight room (below) where players work on strength and conditioning.

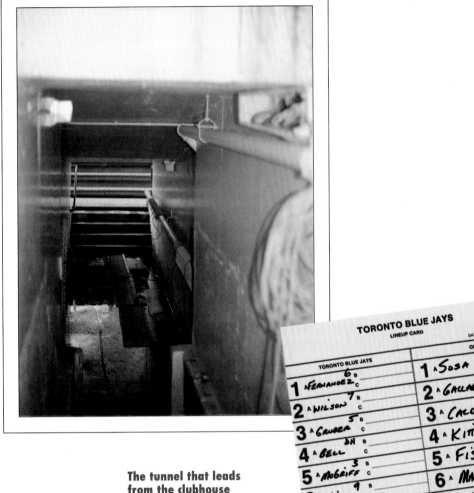

The tunnel that leads from the clubhouse to the dugout (above).

While inside the visitors' dugout, sneak a peek at their line-up card (right).

72

Locker of the manager for the visiting team's clubhouse.

These lockers are spoken for in the visiting team's clubhouse — (right) for Nolan Ryan of the Texas Rangers, and (below), for Bo Jackson of the Kansas City Royals.

Sox Take a Turn for the Worse on "Turn Back the Clock" Day

O n this sunny afternoon, the White Sox are hosting "Turn Back the Clock" Day, returning to baseball as it was played circa 1917 — the last year the Sox won a world series. The game features 50-cent general admission tickets, as well as a manually operated scoreboard and a megaphone announcer. Popcorn is being sold for a nickel while an organ grinder and monkey amuse the crowd.

The Sox are wearing 1917 replica uniforms. The fans were encouraged to come in period dress, which many have. Ushers and other Comiskey personnel are also wearing straw hats, white shirts, bow ties and other appropriate apparel. Nancy Faust plays the accordion today.

It is a gala affair to the delight of 40,666 spectators in attendance.

Everything is perfect as the Sox build a commanding 9-3 lead over the visiting Milwaukee Brewers. However, a disastrous eighth inning sees the Brewers rally for six runs to tie the game and quiet the revelry.

The grounds crew, attired in circa 1917 clothing, prepare the infield on "Turn Back the Clock" Day.

74

Six Sox pitchers participate in the 28-hit game that drags on for 13 long innings. Four hours and 44 minutes go by until the Sox succumb to the victorious Brewers, 12-9. *Say it ain't so, Joe!* ■

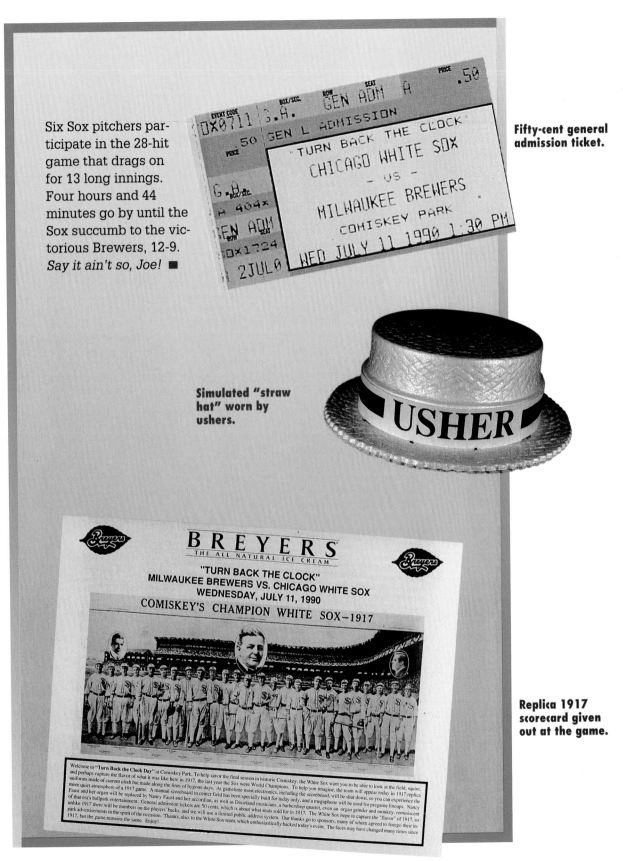

Fifty-cent general admission ticket.

Simulated "straw hat" worn by ushers.

Replica 1917 scorecard given out at the game.

HIGHWAYS AND BYWAYS

Comiskey was nothing, if not cavernous. It was a massive structure with a maze of stairways, ramps and corridors. Often the walkways were dark, damp and seemingly endless. A stroll through Comiskey was an adventure in concrete and steel. But like a favorite old car from your childhood, Comiskey was big, yet quaint and comfortable. True fans knew that each step along the dank and dimly lit corridors was a walk through baseball history.

**Large ramps aid
the traffic flow to
the upper deck.**

A spooky entrance to the field of dreams.

**One of Comiskey's
dimly lit, damp and
seemingly endless
cavities.**

Any spelunker would feel right at home in Old Comiskey.

82

Making the rounds to the concession stands and entrance ramps (left).

Up, up, up the stairs to the upper deck (below).

**One fan waits
patiently while
others crowd the
concession areas.**

84

**Stairway to nowhere.
Don't try exiting here
— this revolving
doorway has long
been abandoned.**

AUGUST 12TH

Rain Delay Forces One Less Home Game for Sox

Today's game against the Texas Rangers is scheduled to begin at 1:35 p.m., but, thanks to a steady, all-day rain, the game never starts and is officially called off at 8:58 p.m. This has been a soggy, seven-hour, 23-minute rain delay that might well be a major league record, if records were kept on such things.

Because the lineup cards are never exchanged, the fate of the game remains in the hands of the home team management, rather than the umpires. The White Sox front office apparently waits as long as possible to call the game because its only alternative is to make the game up in Texas as part of a double-header this coming Friday.

This means the Sox will lose the home field advantage, as well as the home field revenues. The Rangers have refused to make the game up on Thursday at Comiskey, which is an off day for both teams.

At 8:15 p.m., the Sox offer free food to the few hundred wet fans remaining in the ball park. The game is finally called and rescheduled for Friday in Texas.

Because of this quirky turn of events, the White Sox will play 82 road games in 1990, but only 80 home games during this final season at Old Comiskey.

Whenever the rains fall, Comiskey's grounds crew is quick to cover the infield with the tarp.

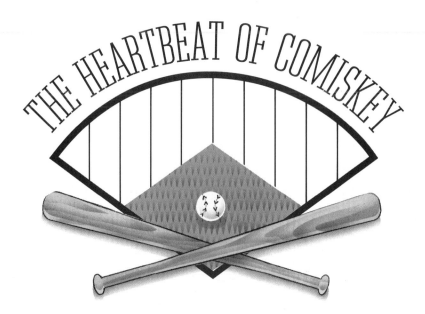

THE HEARTBEAT OF COMISKEY

To understand the charm that made Comiskey Park such a special place to be on a summer's night, it is imperative to look beyond the physical structure of the park itself. Go beyond the walls, the rooms, the hallways and the field. Deep within the confines of Old Comiskey beat a heart. That heartbeat was the people who worked at Comiskey — the dedicated individuals who, game after game, helped make each fan's trip to the ball park a special experience.

88

Outside Comiskey, fans dance and are entertained by street musicians playing "Tequila."

Ordinary empty cans are transformed into the rhythm section.

90

For years, Andy the Clown was the favorite unofficial mascot of Old Comiskey Park. Andy was famous for his ardent cheerleading, "COME ON, you White Sox!"

He also had a reputation as quite the ladies' man. Perhaps it was his irresistible light-up red nose or the long-stemmed red rose he graciously would give to ladies at the park. However, there was a string attached to this gentlemanly act — Andy would walk away with the flower's bud while his unwary admirer was left holding just the stem.

Andy the Clown was honored before the September 28th game. He was given a plaque and a souvenir grandstand seat from Old Comiskey Park in recognition of his 30 years of service at the ball park. Nancy Faust played – what else? – "Send in the Clowns."

(Below) A baseball autographed by Andy "the Clown" Rozdilsky.

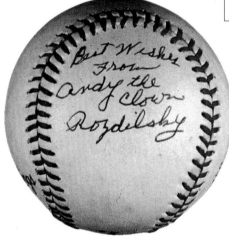

Best Wishes
From
Andy the
Clown
Rozdilsky

92

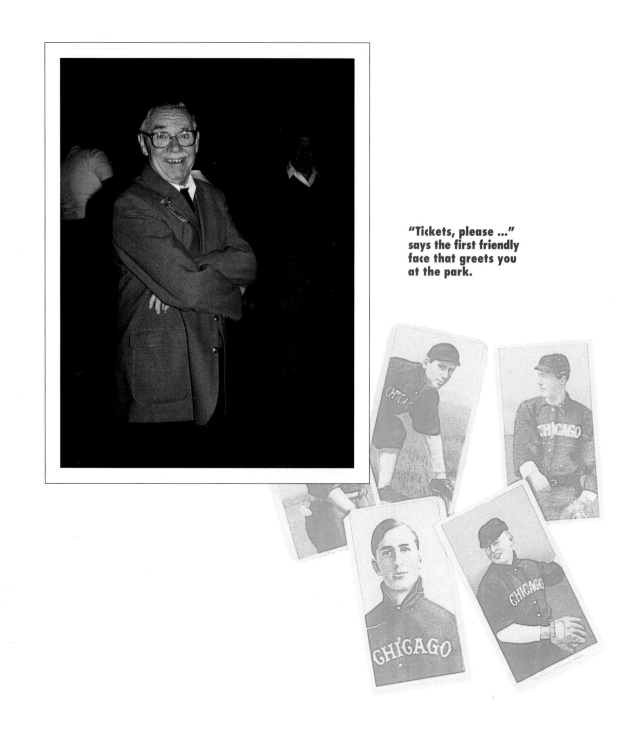

"Tickets, please ..."
says the first friendly
face that greets you
at the park.

GATE 5

IF YOU LEAVE BALL PARK YOU MAY NOT RE-ENTER

IT IS ILLEGAL TO CARRY BEER OUTSIDE OF THE PARK

Two gate attendants (right) make sure no one takes alcoholic beverages out of Comiskey, and, as every fan knows, "If you leave the ball park, you may not re-enter" (above).

94

A Sox security patrol-
man (above) ensures
the fans are protect-
ed from trouble out-
side the ball park.

Andy Frain ushers
(left) await the many
fans they will show to
their seats today.

Two Sox security officers reveal that they are also Sox fans as well, by the collection of souvenir pins on their hats.

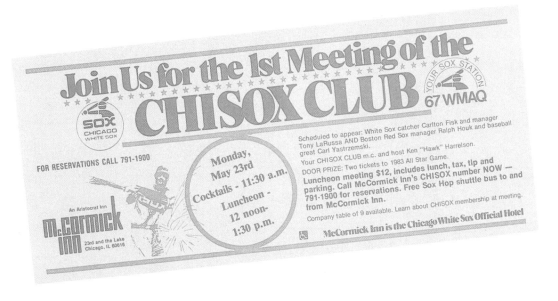

96

Television and radio broadcasters (left) brought White Sox games into the homes of Chicago fans who couldn't make it to the park.

Color commentator Tom Paciorek teamed up with Ken Harrelson or Jim Durham for TV audiences, while John Rooney and Wayne Hagin called the action on the radio side of the booth. Spanish-speaking listeners tuned their radios in to hear Chico Carrasquel and Frank Diaz call the Sox games play-by-play.

(Below) The center field TV camera in front of the bleachers focuses in on the action at home plate.

**Security guards
enjoy the game
while keeping an
eye out for any
trouble.**

98

**The greatest players
ever to play for the
White Sox were
immortalized on the
right field wall of
Comiskey. Players
whose numbers were
retired include:**

**No. 2 Nellie Fox
No. 3 Harold Baines
No. 4 Luke Appling
No. 9 Minnie Minoso
No. 11 Luis Aparicio
No. 16 Ted Lyons
No. 19 Billy Pierce**

On a good night, Comiskey's emergency medical staff (left) gets to enjoy a full game, but just in case they're needed, a nearby stretcher (below) stands ready.

99

100

Rain or shine. Roger Bossard leads his grounds crew in hosing down the field (left) and rolling out the infield tarp (below). Bossard is a third-generation head grounds keeper for the Sox. He also has acted as a consultant for many other major league teams.

Local celebrities were a common sight around Comiskey Park, but few drew as much attention as Chicago Bulls basketball star Michael Jordan. Jordan, a baseball player in high school, was invited to take batting practice with the Sox. To the crowd's delight, he drove several balls into the stands. And to think, he can play *golf* well, too!

Pennant Fever,
Fisk Tribute Excite Chicago Fans

The hottest ticket in town this week gets you into Comiskey Park. The defending world champions, the Oakland Athletics, are in town for their last series of the year at Comiskey against the White Sox. The A's are the only team standing in the way between the surprising second-place White Sox and the top spot in the A.L. West Division.

Large crowds were common in the 1990 season. In some games, stairways served as general admission seats.

August 20

Tonight, pitcher Jack McDowell of the Sox will face Oakland's Dave Stewart. Many of the Comiskey fans are waving jock straps in retaliation to Stewart's comments earlier in the year (after a tough loss) to the effect that most of the Sox players couldn't "carry my jock."

It has rained heavily all day and the field is totally awash. Oakland scores one run in the first inning on a Jose Canseco RBI double. However, the Sox battle back to score three runs in their half of the first inning.

Oakland center fielder Dave Henderson leaves the game after spraining his knee sliding through standing water while chasing a Carlton Fisk RBI bloop single. The game is held up while the grounds crew attempts to dry the field.

The Sox score two more runs in the sixth inning on Sammy Sosa's upper-deck homer. They also score once more in the seventh inning off Stewart, but add five big

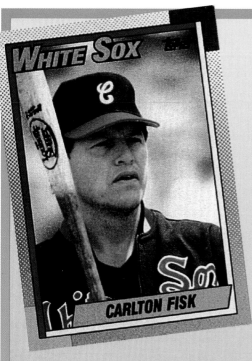

CARLTON FISK

runs off reliever Reggie Harris in the eighth. The huge crowd cheers wildly as each run crosses the plate.

The Oakland ninth brings superstar Jose Canseco to the plate, accompanied by intense booing from the stands. The boos grow louder with each weak tap foul that dinks off his bat. However, the next swing of his bat silences the crowd as the loudest "hit" of the year screams through the night sky over the left field roof near the foul pole. The crowd holds its breath until the umpire confirms that the ball was foul. Canseco whiffs at the next pitch. Put a "K" on the board for a strikeout and Canseco can "grab some bench." The crowd

is once again happy and talkative.

McDowell works all nine innings, throwing a three-hitter. The Sox win 11-1, so Oakland's lead is now cut to only 5½ games.

In the locker room afterwards, McDowell comments on Canseco's power display. "It's the farthest ball I've ever seen hit, and I'm sure 30,000 people think the same thing. I don't know how you could tell that ball was fair or foul. I think it went over the roof on its way up. I don't think it even hit the roof," he says.

August 21

Once again, a packed Comiskey Park rollicks with pennant fever as the White Sox take on the Athletics.

The fans are not disappointed. With Greg Hibbard pitching for Chicago, the Sox and A's play to a 1-1 tie by the bottom half of the seventh inning. However, in that frame, the Sox load up the bases. Up to the plate steps Carlton Fisk, pinch hitting for a pinch hitter as the managers work their strategies.

Despite popular belief, the towering, tape measure foul ball (above) hit by Jose Canseco on August 20 retained its cover.

As the crowd roars with each pitch, Fisk takes aim and pulls a stinging line drive down the third base line. All three base runners score while Fisk stops at second base.

Old Comiskey is literally rocked from the cheers as faithful Sox fans begin to dare dreaming of a world series as a going-away present for the old ball yard.

Although the White Sox have closed the gap to 4½ games behind Oakland, this will prove to be the closest the team gets to first place for the rest of the season. The Sox will end the year with 94 victories and 68 defeats, finishing in second place, nine games behind the Athletics.

August 22

Following last night's heroics, it seems only fitting that today has been declared "Carlton Fisk Day" throughout Chicago and Illinois. In pre-game ceremonies, Fisk is honored with a photo plaque of his most memorable career highlights, a gold watch, and a specially-designed ring.

In a short speech from the field, "Pudge" thanks his current manager, Jeff Torborg, as well as his former manager, Tony LaRussa, currently the manager for tonight's opponent, the Athletics.

Earlier in the week, Fisk had broken two records with one swing of his bat in Arlington, Texas. He hit a home run off Texas Ranger pitcher Charlie Hough. It marked Fisk's 328th career home run as a catcher, the most of any catcher in major league history. The record had previously been held by Johnny Bench.

The homer was also Fisk's 187th as a White Sox player, the most of any player in the franchise's history. He broke Harold Baines' record.

Unfortunately, the pre-game ceremonies will prove to be the

evening's highlight for the Sox, and for Fisk, who does not play in the game.

The ball park, which lists its capacity at 44,000, is jammed with 47,122 fans clamoring for a series sweep of the Athletics. Instead, the Sox' winning streak comes to an end as Oakland's Bob Welch (soon to be the A.L. Cy Young Award winner) picks up his 21st win of the season, defeating the Sox 7-1.

Oakland manager LaRussa, who spent many good years here managing the White Sox, waxes sentimental as he visits Comiskey Park for the last time.

He later confesses he spent the "entire top and bottom of the ninth inning just looking around."

"I was remembering the Bull (Greg Luzinski), Pudge (Fisk) and Harold (Baines) hitting all those home runs," he says. ∎

A Carlton Fisk autographed ball (above).

A full house at Comiskey watch the Sox take on the Oakland Athletics.

Bill Veeck has been widely credited with bringing both the high quality and immense diversity of food to Comiskey Park when he was the White Sox owner. At each home game, a corps of enthusiastic, hard-working vendors served the best food of any ball park in America to White Sox fans. What would a baseball game have been without the familiar cries of "red hots!", "cold beer!" and "Hey, who's hungry for some peanuts!"

108

Soft, giant pretzels were one of the hottest sellers at Comiskey (left).

Hungry for fresh popcorn? You could find it under the stands behind home plate (below).

Cool down with ice cream on a hot afternoon.

110

A beer vendor counts the change for a thirsty customer.

Roll out the barrel (left).

Upper deck aisle service (below).

112

**Stacks of empty beer
cans attest to a busy
day for vendors.**

Step up for a beer,
wine or a hot dog.

113

114

**Cotton candy was
available in the
Picnic Area.**

The vendor loading station (above) was located under the stands on the park's south side. This area was once the site of the Sox' own bottling plant that has long since been dismantled.

A bottle of the White Sox' orange soda, (left) produced at the Comiskey bottling plant.

116

A hot dog vendor
sells a "red hot" to
a hungry fan.

Fans wait outside
the gate (right) even
before the program
vendor has arrived.

A souvenir stand
(below) awaits cus-
tomers from beyond
Comiskey's fences.

118

Sox fans could buy
more than just food
and drink at Comiskey.
Souvenir stands sold
everything from caps,
pennants and batting
gloves to Sox pitcher
Jack McDowell's rock
band's cassette tape.

Outside the ball park, street vendors hawk t-shirts, including 1990's popular Bart Simpson shirts.

120

Inside this dressing room, vendors change from ordinary citizens to a most welcome sight for hungry and thirsty White Sox patrons.

Thigpen Breaks
Single-Season Record

A nother White Sox star sets a major league record when reliever Bobby Thigpen picks up his 47th save of the year against the Kansas City Royals. With his one inning of scoreless work, he sets the all-time record for saves in a single season.

Thigpen's record not only reflects on his own excellent pitching talents, but also on the fact that he plays for a team that wins a lot of very close ball games. Just getting the opportunity to save more than 50 games in a season is remark-able. Yet, low-scoring, close games are the standard operating procedure for the 1990 Sox.

The following evening, Thigpen is honored at Comiskey Park in a pre-game ceremony. As announcer Ken "Hawk" Harrelson would put it—*"YES!"* ■

'90 SCORE

BOBBY THIGPEN RP

Among the highlights of the 1990 season for Sox fans was witnessing the record number of saves by Bobby Thigpen.

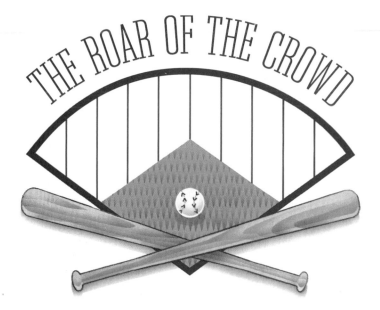

THE ROAR OF THE CROWD

It is the fans who
buy the tickets, buy the food and buy
the souvenirs. It is the fans who yell
and cheer for the players on the field.
It is the fans who come to the games
and carry those precious moments
with them all their lives. Fans are
the key element in the success of
any sports franchise. Without White
Sox fans, there would be no White
Sox team. It is the fans who care.

124

Fans cheer for the hometown favorite team from opposite sides of Comiskey Park: from the left field bleachers (left) and from behind home plate (below).

The buildings of Armour Square peek over the shoulders of upper deck fans. Although considered a South Side team, Sox fans came to Comiskey from every neighborhood of Chicago and the suburbs, as well as from across the country.

126

Fans show their continued support of "Shoeless" Joe Jackson (left), who was banned from major league base-ball after the 1919 "Black Sox" world series scandal.

Other Sox faithful root for their team to overtake the Oakland A's for the West Division title (below). However, the White Sox ended their brief stint in first place during the last week of June, and the Athletics held on to clinch the divi-sion on September 25.

The last row of the right field grandstand offers these fans shade and a cool breeze on a hot summer's day.

128

Fans gathered at Comiskey (left) always had at least one shared interest — to "root, root, root" for the White Sox.

"Camera Night" on September 26th gave fans a chance to take snapshots of White Sox players modeling their new 1991 uniforms.

Sox newcomer, Matt Stark, still awaiting his number 21 to be sewn on his jersey, poses with a fan (below).

Because 1990 was the final season at Old Comiskey Park, the usual assortment of promotional gifts to fans took on special meaning as keepsakes from "The Great Lady" at 35th and Shields.

SEPTEMBER 28TH

Security Beefed Up for
Final Weekend at Comiskey

Despite afternoon rain showers, the White Sox begin their final home series of the year with a Friday night game. The temperature hovers at 64 degrees as more than 37,000 fans witness a White Sox loss to the Seattle Mariners, 13-4. Randy Johnson will go the distance for Seattle, while the Sox send Alex Fernandez, Steve Rosenberg, Donn Pall, Scott Radinsky and Shawn Hillegas to the mound.

The last Sox home run hit at Old Comiskey will come tonight off the bat of rookie Frank Thomas, who tees off on a pitch in the second inning and sends it into the left-center field stands. "Put it on the board!" cheers Ken Harrelson.

By late August, all signs and photographs under the stands have been taken down by Sox management to remove any temptation to memorabilia hunters. The plan is to make all of the items available to the fans through charity auction.

Afternoon rain showers dampen the field, but not the enthusiasm of 37,000 fans who will show up for the final Friday night game at Old Comiskey.

Nevertheless, some fans grab handfuls of warning track gravel or small chips of the Great Lady's walls. There are even a few instances reported of fans trying to remove the *pièce de résistance* — complete seats.

Security is beefed up daily in and around the park as the final game approaches. Mounted police begin to appear on the field after each game of the final weekend series. ■

**AISLE 259
SEC 242-3**

White Sox management ordered the removal of all signs (above left) and photographs to protect them from souvenir collectors.

Additional security measures are added at Comiskey (top and right) just in case the large crowds get out of hand. However, White Sox fans behaved in exemplary fashion all weekend.

COMISKEY AFTER DARK

When the sun went down, the arc lights went on high above Comiskey Park. The lights brightened the neighborhood and could be seen for miles around Chicago. In 1990, the 17-year cicadas chirped a chorus while the usual collection of flying insects circled frantically around the lights. The light standards shone like a beacon, calling all faithful Chicago White Sox fans to the South Side for that night's game.

134

**Lights were origi-
nally added to
Comiskey in 1939,
giving fans who
work during the
day a better chance
to attend games.**

WATCH
THE
FIGHTING WHITE SOX

With storm clouds gathering in the distance, the new Comiskey Park waits on deck for its turn in 1991.

136

On the South Side of
Chicago, residents
would run out to
their front porches
or peer through
their windows at
the sound of fire-
works because it
meant a home run
or other celebration
at Old Comiskey.

One reason Chicago-
ans associate night
baseball so strongly
with Old Comiskey
Park is that for
nearly 50 years it
was the only base-
ball park in town
with lights. Wrigley
Field didn't install
lights until 1988.

Turning Off the Lights Turns on the Tears at the Final Night Game

138

More than 42,000 fans jam Comiskey Park to witness the last-ever night game in the old ball park.

On Saturday, 42,800 fans fill Comiskey for the last-ever night game to be played here. Tonight's starting pitchers are Eric King for the Sox versus Seattle's Matt Young.

Seattle gets on the scoreboard first in the fourth inning with Alvin Davis' two-run home run into the right field stands. This is the last homer ever to be hit in Old Comiskey Park.

The Sox' fourth inning produces one run when Robin Ventura's single drives in Sammy Sosa from second base. But the two decisive runs come in the seventh inning when "awesome" Frank Thomas singles with the bases loaded, driving in Ventura and Scott Fletcher.

The Sox get another run home when Phil Bradley scores on a wild pitch by Seattle's Mike Jackson. The Sox' fifth run comes in the eighth inning when Ron Karkovice scores on a sacrifice fly by Fletcher. The Sox will back up Eric King's effort with Barry Jones and Bobby Thigpen, who records his 56th save as the Sox defeat the Mariners 5-2.

The first-ever night game took place at Comiskey Park on August 14, 1939. By coincidence, the Sox were victorious over the St. Louis Browns by the identical score of 5-2.

After the game, amid hundreds of security personnel and mounted police on the field, Charles A. Comiskey II, together with a contest-winning fan, ceremoniously pull the switch to turn out the lights for the last

time. Interestingly, it was Comiskey, only a child at the time, who turned on the lights for the first night game back in 1939.

After the game, mounted police (above) ring the field for the post-game "Turn out the Lights" ceremony.

The switch was pulled by Charles Comiskey II and a fan and out went the lights (left).

In the darkness, there is an eerie moment of silence as thousands of flashbulbs go off. The once-festive fans turn somber, realizing what they have witnessed. They begin to chant, "na na na na, hey hey hey, goodbye." Rooftop fireworks begin Comiskey Park's last and largest fireworks display ever.

At 10:14 p.m., the lights are turned back on a smoke-filled Comiskey Park for easier exiting and public safety.

An eerie moment of silence overtook the melancholic crowd....

...until fireworks filled the air and broke the silence.

The mass law enforcement is not necessary as most fans leave without incidence. Night baseball at Comiskey Park has faded into the past. Grown men can be seen crying in the aisles. ■

The lights were turned back on for safe exiting (left), but no one seemed to be in a hurry to leave. Many fans just wanted to stand and savor the significance of the moment.

(Below)"Thanks for the memories, Comiskey Park, 1910-1990."

SEPTEMBER 30th

Fans, Players Say "Goodbye" to Comiskey Park at Final Game

On a beautiful September Sunday afternoon, the White Sox will play their final game ever in Old Comiskey Park.

On Sunday morning, fans begin to gather around Comiskey hours before game time. It is the start of a picture-perfect day with winds out of the northwest at 16 m.p.h. Game time temperatures will reach 62 degrees. The Oak Ridge Boys can be heard practicing the national anthem from within the ball park.

There are tailgate parties and it seems as if every fan has a camera or videocam, if not both. Souvenirs are selling fast, especially the final game program. Game tickets can still be purchased outside the park from scalpers — if you're willing to pay the going price of 50 bucks.

Comiskey's northern neighbor, Armour Square Park, still heavily littered with fireworks wrappers from last night, plays host to a going-away party.

The mood in the air is festive, yet there is that strong feeling of nostalgia. All of the fans seem keenly aware of the significance of today's game.

A tranquil crowd waits at each of Comiskey's gates for the last announcement of, "The gates to the ball park will now open." It comes at approximately 11:30 a.m. Certificates with a slot for a ticket stub are handed to fans as they enter.

Once inside, fans form a continuous stream in the aisleways, trying to get their last looks or final photographs. Some sit in treasured seats, stirring memories of times past. You can detect it in their quiet, faraway stares.

A Chicago policeman stands motionless in the upper deck, holding his half-eaten hot dog while a song that seems to provoke a memory is playing. A melancholic atmosphere permeates the stands.

Gourmets of Comiskey cuisine scramble to the concessions for one last taste. People bid farewell to ball park friends

they have made during this and many other seasons. Andy the Clown draws perhaps the largest crowd of well-wishers. Banners of all descriptions adorn Comiskey's walls. Short-stop Ozzie Guillen stands in center field throwing baseballs into the stands as parting gifts.

The Oak Ridge Boys' rendition of the national anthem is sung

A large pre-game party (above) in Armour Square Park celebrates 80 years of its most famous neighbor — Old Comiskey.

The hottest ticket in Chicago sports lets you through the gates to witness the end of an era (left).

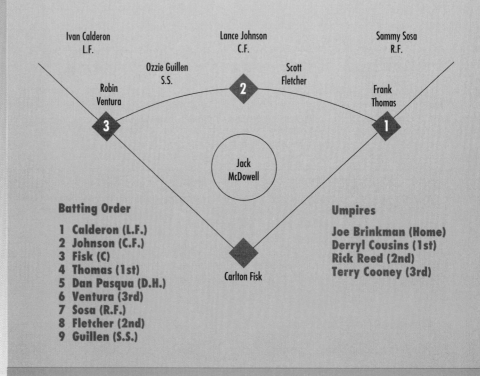

My place in history

was present at the Final Game in historic Comiskey Park. Sunday, September 30, 1990.

On behalf of the Chicago White Sox and my grandfather, who built Comiskey Park in 1910, I'd like to thank you for coming. It has been a glorious run.

Charles A. Comiskey II

This limited edition certificate is one of only 47,000 printed, the total attendance at the Final Game.

Certificates were distributed at the gates to fans. A slot for a ticket stub would prove you were there for the final game at Old Comiskey.

with authority and wets many an eye. Mayor Richard M. Daley throws out the first ball while Charles A. Comiskey II stands nearby.

Wearing his retired uniform number 9, honorary team captain Minnie Minoso delivers the starting lineups to home plate umpire Joe Brinkman. A standing ovation ensues.

Minutes later, the White Sox take the field to the thunderous ovations that have been so well earned this season. Yet another round of cheers and a standing ovation greet catcher Carlton Fisk as he takes the field for the last time at Old Comiskey Park.

As the Sox warm up, even the first base umpire Derryl Cousins videotapes the event. More than one video camera can also be seen peeking out of the dugouts.

Helicopters and small airplanes carrying "Goodbye Comiskey" banners begin their game-long buzz overhead.

Ivan Calderon L.F.

Lance Johnson C.F.

Sammy Sosa R.F.

Ozzie Guillen S.S.

Scott Fletcher

Robin Ventura

Frank Thomas

2

3

1

Jack McDowell

Carlton Fisk

Batting Order

1 Calderon (L.F.)
2 Johnson (C.F.)
3 Fisk (C)
4 Thomas (1st)
5 Dan Pasqua (D.H.)
6 Ventura (3rd)
7 Sosa (R.F.)
8 Fletcher (2nd)
9 Guillen (S.S.)

Umpires

Joe Brinkman (Home)
Derryl Cousins (1st)
Rick Reed (2nd)
Terry Cooney (3rd)

The table has been set and two teams are ready to play a baseball game, but it will be the spirits of Old Comiskey Park that will have control over today's game.

Sox pitcher Jack McDowell retires the first batter, Harold Reynolds, on three consecutive pitches as he goes down swinging to the delight of the capacity 42,849 on hand. McDowell retires the side and then it is Seattle pitcher Rick DeLucia's turn on the mound.

Mayor Daley has his moment in the sun when a third-inning pop foul slips through his outstretched hands.

In the fourth inning, actor John Candy, one of the many celebrities on hand, does a stint as a play-by-play announcer, joining Tom Paciorek and Ken Harrelson in the television broadcasting booth.

Seattle gets its only run in the sixth inning when Ken Griffey, Jr., who has led off with a triple comes in on a wild pitch. Both Sox runs also score in the sixth, as Lance Johnson (3 for 3) leads off with a triple. Big Frank Thomas promptly singles to center, bringing Johnson home. Thomas scores as Dan Pasqua knocks a "bad-hop" triple that squeezes past Ken Griffey, Sr. in left field.

Sadly, there will be no more runs ever scored at Old Comiskey Park. (Although the game did offer several more close calls....)

145

Beer sales are permanently cut off in the fifth inning (above).

The final game scorecard (left) was in big demand as a momento.

Seattle's Dave Valle leads off the seventh with a double into the right field corner, but he's thrown out trying for third base.

The seventh inning stretch features the local singing group, Styx, who come out onto the field to lead the crowd in the last rendition of "Take Me Out to the Ballgame."

Ken Griffey, Jr. leads off the eighth inning with a deep fly ball that drives Lance Johnson all the way to the center field wall before he records the out. Greg Briley comes in to run for

Alvin Davis, who doubled. Tino Martinez strikes out and the third out comes when left fielder Ivan Calderon makes a graceful running backhanded stab of a sinking line drive off the bat of Jay Buhner, saving a run.

In the Sox' half of the eighth, Fisk receives another standing ovation after he fouls out to the first baseman—his final at bat at Old Comiskey. The fans, wanting Fisk back out of the dugout, first see Ozzie Guillen jokingly take the curtain call before Fisk consents to step out of the dugout and tip his cap to the cheering crowd.

The climactic ninth inning brings Bobby Thigpen to the mound while Steve Lyons replaces Frank Thomas at first base. The infield shadow continues to slowly creep across the field. The Sox are after their 93rd victory of the season.

First up is pinch hitter Scott Bradley, who singles to right field. When Omar Vizquel tries to advance him to second base with a bunt, Fisk guns down Bradley at second. Pinch hitter Pete O'Brien flies out to left-center field and, finally, Harold Reynolds, who had been today's first batter two

Organist Nancy Faust warms up as respectful fans file past.

TODAY WE HONOR THE OLDEST BALLPARK IN THE MAJOR LEAGUES

hours and 43 minutes earlier, grounds the ball to Scott Fletcher at second base. Fletcher fields the ball, throws it to Lyons at first base and more than 80 years of Comiskey Park history comes to an end at 4:23 p.m.

Security forces immediately flood the field in anticipation of the exuberant behavior fans have exhibited when other famous ball parks have closed. Sox security is joined by 175 uniformed police, some of whom are mounted on horses. Two paddy wagons come in from the bullpen. The crowd remains in the stands, despite the challenge, perhaps too reverent to step on hallowed ground.

Meanwhile, Sox players congratulate each other on their 2-1 victory and head into the dugout. However, in response to the considerate fan behavior and the calls for an encore, the Sox players soon return to the field. A few fireworks are set off and "Na Na Na Na, Hey Hey Hey, Goodbye" is played for the last time as the Sox tour the field, bidding their farewells.

Nancy Faust officially makes "Auld Lang Syne" her last selection. The players all too soon drop out of sight one by one into the dugout. Appropriately, Fisk is the last to leave the field.

After the game, an Andy Frain usher proposes to his girlfriend at home plate. She answers, "Yes!"

Head grounds keeper Roger Bossard has the solemn task of removing home plate and the pitching rubber where, minutes before, Thigpen recorded his record-establishing 57th save of the year.

Seattle Mariners manager Jim Lefebvre comments on the game, lamenting, "The gods of baseball were on their side today."

Dan Pasqua (below) hit a triple in the final game.

As most fans move toward the exits, some remain in their seats, misty eyed while collecting their memories. A serenity settles over Comiskey that has never before been experienced — a Comiskey that will be forever empty.

Reynolds grounds out to second base — the final out of the game (above).

The bullpens empty followed by the mounted police and two paddy wagons (left).

148

"Thank you for attending the final game to be held here at Comiskey Park. The gates to historic Comiskey Park, the baseball palace of the world, are in the process of being locked for one final time," came the announcement over the public address system.

Goodbye to the old. Hello to the new.

Goodbye old friend. ■

White Sox players (above) congratulate each other after the victory.

The security force hired to keep fans off the field is not needed as the fans prefer to stay in the stands and reminisce (left).

GOODBYE OLD FRIEND

During its eighty years, Old Comiskey Park's fans experienced almost every emotion possible to mankind. From the exuberance of the park's opening in 1910, to the frustration of last-place finishes, Sox fans have been through it all. But on September 30, 1990, a new and different emotion settled over Comiskey's stands. The fans knew they were witnessing the end of an era —that today they must say goodbye forever to an old friend.

MARK!!
9/13/90
I came from Reading, PA!
THE SOX ARE GREAT!!!
RENATA KEVIN
ARMANDO DAN '90
DIANA
John
A'S Suck
CHRIS K
Gina Cortesi
11-2-90
Jeremy

152

Many fans were slow to leave their seats, preferring to reflect upon their last visit to Old Comiskey Park.

153

"Goodbye to the old.
Hello to the new."

154

4:59 p.m., September
30, 1990, and the
ball park is emptied
of fans.

**Solemn fans pay
their last respects
(right).**

**The final exit
(below).**

156

**The writing on the
wall – goodbye to
80 years of history.**

Goodbye, old friend.
Goodbye forever.

157

About the Author

"Years from now, you will say you were there."

That was the slogan used by the Chicago White Sox to urge fans to buy tickets for the 1990 baseball season — the final season ever for Old Comiskey Park.

One fan in particular took that slogan to heart and began his one-man mission to preserve that feeling of being there for the historic last season.

Frank Budreck attended every White Sox home game in 1990. From the box seats to the bleachers, he took hundreds of photographs and scribbled down page after page of notes. His goal was to accurately capture not only the significant baseball events, but also the feelings and emotions of Comiskey Park's last hurrah.

Frank is neither a professional photographer nor a professional writer. He is simply a lifelong devoted White Sox fan who grew up on the South Side of Chicago, virtually in the shadow of the great ball park.

His earliest memories of Comiskey Park spring from his childhood in the early 1960s. They include the tremendous crowds that would always show up to watch the Sox do battle with the hated and great New York Yankee teams of that era, and the vociferous Andy the Clown.

Since those days, Budreck has attended hundreds of games at Comiskey Park. Some of his most memorable moments there include the 50th Anniversary All-Star game played in 1983 and the division-clinching game on September 17th of that same year.

He has been lucky enough to be at the ball park to witness quite a few of the rooftop home run blasts — always an exciting moment at Comiskey. He also survived possibly the strangest night ever at Comiskey — the infamous "Disco Demolition" on July 12, 1979.

Frank is a member of the ChiSox Club and the Society for American Baseball Research (S.A.B.R.). He now makes his home in a western suburb of Chicago.

Your Personal Memories/Autographs